Carrying

Gwenyth Swain

Lerner Publications Company/Minneapolis

small world

For my father, G. Henry Swain, who used to carry me on his shoulders

To find out more about the pictures in this book, turn to page 22.
To find out more about sharing this book with children, turn to page 24.

The photographs in this book are reproduced through the courtesy of: ELCA photo library. Used by permission of Augsburg Fortress, front cover, p. 20; © John Elk III, back cover, p. 21; © Elaine Little/World Photo Images, pp. 1, 4; © Lyn Hancock, p. 3; Red Sea Mission Team, Inc., p. 5; © Gerald Cubitt, p. 6; Aramco World Magazine, p. 7; © Trip/M Jelliffe, pp. 8, 16; Heinz Kluetmeier/Dot Photos, p. 9; Piotr Kostrzewski/Cross Cultural Adventures, p. 10; World Bank Photo, p. 11; Jim Hubbard, p. 12; © Lyn Hancock, p. 13; Laurie Nelson, p. 14; Agency for International Development, p. 15; Hans Olaf Pfannkuch, p. 17; Photo Action USA, Cy White, p. 18; Ray Witlin; World Bank Photo, p. 19.

First Avenue Editions, an imprint of Lerner Publishing Group, Inc.
241 First Avenue North, Minneapolis, MN 55401 U.S.A.

Website address: www.lernerbooks.com

Library of Congress Cataloging-in-Publication Data

Swain, Gwenyth, 1961–
   Carrying / by Gwenyth Swain.
      p.   cm. — (Small world)
   Includes index.
   Summary: Explores the importance of carrying things as well as babies and of lending
a helping hand by sharing a load.
   ISBN-13: 978-1-57505-373-8 (pbk. : alk. paper)
   ISBN-10: 1-57505-373-X (pbk. : alk. paper)
1. Sharing—Juvenile literature. 2. Lifting and carrying—Juvenile literature.
[1. Sharing 2. Lifting and carrying.] I. Title. II. Series: Small world (Minneapolis, Minn.)
BF575.S48S93   1999
179.'9—dc21   98-3755

Manufactured in the United States of America
6 7 8 9 10 11 – JR – 13 12 11 10 09 08

What do you carry?

Do you carry your books
on the way to school?

Do you carry your shoes
when you need to stay cool?

The things we carry can be very large

or very small.

We carry sticks for a fire

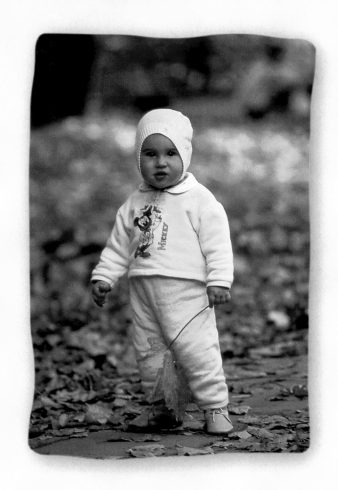

and colored leaves in fall.

Does someone, sometimes,
carry you?

Often, the people who care for us,
carry us, too!

A mother with babies
has much to hold.

But she'll have help from her children
when she grows old.

Carrying means sharing a load,

bringing food to the table,
or moving down the road.

When you carry things for others,

you lend a helping hand.

Carrying lifts the spirit

and makes us strong.

It makes a long road short.

It tells us we belong.

More about the Pictures

Front cover: In Cameroon, a country in West Africa, two girls carry babies—one real and one a doll.

Back cover: A young boy at a monastery in India holds a key.

Page 1: A boy carries fish to the market on Jolo, an island in the Philippines.

Page 3: An Inuit girl carries her doll on her back in Nunavut, a territory in northern Canada.

Page 4: In the Philippines, a boy brings his books home from school.

Page 5: A girl carries her shoes and a bucket on a hot day in Mali, a West African country.

Page 6: Girls balance jars full of well water on their heads in Rajasthan in northwestern India.

Page 7: In the desert of Algeria, a country in North Africa, a boy holds a stick toy.

Page 8: A girl in Cameroon brings home wood for the fire.

Page 9: A boy in Russia takes a fallen leaf as his prize.

Page 10: A woman in Mali carefully carries her two babies.

Page 11: In South Korea, an older woman cares for—and carries—a small child.

 Page 12: Twins are a heavy load for this mother in Washington, D.C.

 Page 13: An Inuit woman and her daughter carry children on their backs in Nunavut, Canada.

 Page 14: In Peru, men work together to carry a symbol of the Virgin Mary during Candelaria, a festival.

 Page 15: In Nepal, a girl climbs a steep road while carrying a child.

 Page 16: A girl in Cameroon sells *mandasi* (cooked dough balls).

 Page 17: In Senegal, a country in West Africa, two boys work together to get water from a well.

 Page 18: In Milwaukee, Wisconsin, a clown lifts a little girl above the crowd, lifting her spirits, as well.

 Page 19: A woman in Ethiopia balances a heavy water-filled gourd on her head.

 Page 20: Two young women make a journey together in Cameroon.

 Page 21: Boy Scouts in Bangkok, Thailand, take part in a water-carrying contest.

dults on Sharing This Book

Help your child become a lifelong reader. Read this book together, taking turns as you both read out loud. Look over the photographs and choose your favorites. Sound out new words and come back to them later for review. Then try these "extensions"—activities that extend the experience of reading and build discussion and problem-solving skills.

Talk about Carrying

All around the world, you can find people carrying things—and other people. Discuss with your child the things people carry. How do the people shown in this book carry things? How does your child carry things to school? How do ways of carrying things or people differ? How are they the same?

Carry Things in Different Ways

With your child, gather a few unbreakable objects you can carry, such as a book, a brush, or a backpack. Try carrying each object in three different ways: on or over your shoulder, on your head, and in your hand. Which way of carrying each thing seemed easier or harder? Ask your child why certain objects were easier to carry one way than another.